The Business of Living

The Business of Living

You don't need the key to success if you know how to pick the lock!

Jack Freeman

Caleb Hill Press

CONTENTS

CONTENTS

Introduction

Hi. My name is Jack and I'm truly excited for *you*. You're about to start succeeding in ways you never thought possible. This is a book about success—though "success" is a loaded term and means different things to different people. Instead, I should say that this book is about *getting ahead* because it takes a narrow view of success. If you are looking for spiritual success or growth, stop reading. If you are looking for the answer to, "How can I become a well-rounded person?" Stop reading. If success to you includes, "making the planet a better place," stop reading. I'm not here to coddle you. I'm here to help you make something of yourself. This book is based on my original tape series, *The Business of Living*, which consisted of eighty-five cassette tapes that went on to sell over twelve thousand sets world-wide and I'm proud to be finally bringing it to the English speaking countries.

When I turned in the manuscript of this book to my editor, he voiced some concern about it being such a short volume, coming in at about nine thousand words. I pointed out that the United States Constitution contains only 4,543 words and it does a fine job of getting it's message across. *The Business of Living* is close to *double in size*, and is arguably *just as important* in its own way. If the U. S. Constitution is about creating a successful democracy, then *The Business of Living* is about creating a successful You, and like the Constitution, *The Business of Living* is subject to ongoing debate by scholars as to its intended meaning and relevance.

The Business of Living is a short book because it doesn't need to be long—it's not rocket science! As I say to people everyday, *If they can make penicillin out of moldy bread, then I can make something out of you.*

So let's get down to business—the *business of You.*

Part I: The Success Industry, Political Correctness, & You

What do these three things all have in common? All three are keeping you from being who you are and what you can be.

The Success Industry

Let's take a look at the traditional "success-motivational" industry for a moment. It's a huge industry and there are any number of famous authors and experts to tell you how to make your life better.

Many of them, like me, are household names—but unlike me, these guys are the *elites*. Tony Robinson. Zig Ziglar. Napoleon Hill. But like many elites in our society today, they are out of touch with the common man or woman.

Take Tony Robbins. One of the most recognized self-improvement/motivational speakers in the world, Tony Robbins, wrote a book that over sold 20 million copies called, *Awaken the Giant Within*. In it, he postulates that we all have a "giant" within us, just waiting to break out and accomplish wonderful things.

I believe that's a crock of s**t. I think that if you feel like you have a "giant" within you, you're probably just constipated.

Mr. Robbins also has a trust-building or "empowerment" technique whereby he has people walk barefoot over red-hot coals to increase their self-esteem.

My theories teach you how to afford fireproof shoes.

Let's look at a few more examples. These next two were written almost fifty years ago and are still big best-sellers today.

The first is Napoleon Hill's, *Think and Grow Rich*. A decent book, but thinking is overrated. You can't think your way to riches—you have to DO. *Do* and grow Rich.

Then there's the multi-million-copy seller, Zig Ziglar's *See You at the Top!* A hugely popular book, this has always seemed vague to me. *Where* exactly is the Top? *What* is the Top? The financial Top? The "feel good about yourself" Top? His book conveys an "all or none" attitude—either you're at the top or you're down at the bottom. Instead of *See You at the Top!* how about a book called, *Meet Me in the Middle!.* Sounds a little more attainable to most people.

Of course Jen Sincero is the modern millennial who has written a best seller called *You are a Badass!* This is a newer take on the "the Giant within" theory, except she wants you to embrace your inner badass. But I don't want to be known as a badass—unless cage fighting is my path to riches.

"Okay Jack, you've picked apart the other books—why is yours any different? I mean, *The Business of Living* sounds like just another angle."

That's fair. Except that I won't ever attempt to "pump you up" like some books do. I won't promise to see you at the top and I won't help you find your inner anything. In fact, I seldom look inward. This book doesn't assume that success is some far-off destination or an "all-or-none" proposition. Most other books tend to make success seem elusive.

Along with my philosophy of life being a series of transactions, is my motto "You don't need the key to success if you know how to pick the lock." That means thinking outside of the box—which is your key to successful transactions. I also assume that you may not have access to the traditional key. You may not have been born with advantages that make it easy to get the "key to success." If you can learn to pick the lock, you're thinking on your feet. *You are not beholden to someone who has the key and is dangling it in front of you.*

Now, before going ANY further in this book, I want you to take five minutes and give four or five brief answers on the following two pages. *Use a pen or felt tip marker!*

MY FINANCIAL GOALS

1._____
2._____
3._____
4._____
5._____

MY WEAKNESSES

1._____
2._____
3._____
4._____
5._____

The State of Success in America

As I write this in 2020, it's obvious that we don't live in an America that's conducive to success. And by that I don't mean the economic climate or unemployment rates. I mean the *cultural climate*. Virtually everything today tends to be governed through the lens of Political Correctness. So what does that have to do with this book? Everything.

Because the hallmark of Political Correctness is that it ignores individual differences in people and demands that people ignore any gut instinct or experience they've had in the world around them in an effort to ensure that no one is offended or feels "demeaned." It is cultural tyranny and *one of the main goals of Political Correctness is to prevent excellence from taking place*. Because in the mind of the PC crowd, your excelling or getting ahead means someone else must be getting harmed, put out, or left feeling bad about themselves. At its core, political correctness assumes *that for every person succeeding, someone else is being deprived.* It's about quashing excellence.

Your personal and financial excellence.

Well, PC police, Jack Freeman says, *tough shit*. Because when individuals excel, America excels. So then, how can you excel in this climate of fear and bullying? By completely ignoring political correctness in all its success-crushing forms. It's a dog-eat-dog world out there and no one's going to help you get ahead except you—with a little help from Jack Freeman. By the way, do you know why I had you write your goals down in pen on the proceeding pages? "I assume, Jack, it's because you wanted us to visualize and make manifest our commitment to our dreams!"

No. I had you mark up the book so that you couldn't sell it as "used" on Amazon. That way, people can only buy *new* copies of my book. There's your first lesson.

P.O.W.

I have given thousands of motivational speeches, mostly to myself.—Jack Freeman

The following is from an anonymous letter I received a while back:

> A few years ago, I was watching a news story of an Air Force pilot who'd been shot down in the Middle East and captured. They showed a picture of the young American P.O.W. He was in a tent surrounded by his captors who were jubilant and waving AK47s above their heads. As I stared at him there was something familiar about this prisoner.
>
> It was the look on his face. Though he was trying to look defiant, there was a glimmer of fear in his eyes and maybe a hint of feeling foolish for getting himself into a situation far beyond his training.
>
> I'd seen that look before. *In the mirror.*

It was then I realized that I too, was a P.O.W.—in a war with myself.

Aren't we always our own worst enemy, held against our will by hostile forces—the forces being us?

We hold ourselves back from our potential. Keeping ourselves blindfolded, handcuffed, and hobbled from life's possibilities. We don't even give ourselves the benefit of the Geneva Convention. We beat ourselves up, endure brutal interrogations administered by ourselves, to ourselves.

But unlike that Air Force pilot, nobody has a gun to my head. I can walk out of my prison if I just let myself.

Though instead, I sit in limbo, unsure whether to attempt an escape or just wait until the war within me ends of its own accord. I shouldn't be here—I've done nothing. And yet, I'm not innocent. I'm guilty of crimes against humanity. My own.

A Rude Awakening

Let me ask you. Do you often feel that you're never really successful? You're poised for it, you feel like success is close—but it always seems to be just beyond your reach. Do you feel like you're *stalking success*? Success is like a beautiful woman, and as you follow her down the street, she quickens her step. You call her on the phone and she hangs up and blocks you. You find yourself peering in the window of Success wearing the woolen ski mask of optimism, only to find she has put a restraining order on you.

But maybe you're not stalking success at all. *Maybe success is stalking you and you're keeping one step ahead of it.*

Recently, a friend of mine, Bernie, told me a story that gave great insight into his psyche and how we avoid success. Bernie was sitting in a bar having a drink when he noticed that a very good looking, upscale woman sitting at the other end of the bar was giving him a flirtatious look. She smiled at him and motioned for him to come sit with her. Bernie went over and sat down next to her. For the next half hour they chatted, laughed, and flirted with each other.

So Bernie then says, "You want to play a game called, 'Win a date with Bernie?'"

The woman, deciding to play along, says, "Sure. How do we play?"

Bernie says, "Simple, just pick a number between one and fifty. If you guess the number, we go out on a fantastic, fun-filled date!"

She rolls her eyes and laughs, "Yeah, right. *Any* number I pick is going to be the one you were thinking of."

"C'mon, give me a little credit. Pick one," he replies.

So she thinks for a moment and says, "Okay, the number is thirty-eight."

Bernie looks at her with amazement. "You have to be kidding me—*you picked thirty-eight? The number you chose was thirty-eight?*"

The woman smiles at him skeptically, "Let me guess—that was the number you were thinking of."

"No," Bernie tells her. "The number I was thinking of was thirty-nine—you were so close. Better luck next time." And he gets up and walks away.

What is it that made Bernie say thirty-nine? More importantly, how many times do you say thirty-nine in *your* life?

Like our friend Bernie, I would argue that maybe you're not as successful as you'd like because you have some flaw or fault within you. Yes. It just might be that *you* are your problem.

That is not what you wanted to hear. My assertion certainly goes against current politically correct self-help theories of the human condition, which say, *"You're perfect just the way you are!"*

No, sadly, you are *not* perfect. In fact, you're probably a goddamn mess. You are your own worst enemy and your middle name should be Versus. You're being misled because the Success Establishment today would have you believe that you basically have your shit together and just need a little kick in the butt to achieve Greatness—you just need to set an alarm clock to "Awaken the Giant Within!" Well, let's face it—most of us aren't super-achievers. We're short on self-discipline, self-esteem, and our motivation likely needs a defibrillator just to get jump started.

Which brings us to the concept of *value*. You have two values. You have a value to yourself and a value to others.

You see, most self-help books and current cultural teachings are geared towards upping your value to *yourself*. It's imperative that you see yourself as empowered or relevant and the culture of Political Correctness is in place to insure—*by force*—your value to society at large. This would include everything from quotas, affirmative action, and "emotional intelligence."

But they are artificial valuations. They have to be propped up constantly like an inflated balloon—but like a balloon, as soon as you quit inflating it, the balloon collapses. The first thing you need to do is, *quit putting so much value on yourself.*

It is your value to *others*. In the marketplace of Life that makes you desirable, a sought after product. So the first thing you need to do is quit valuing yourself so much and start looking at your worth through the worlds' eyes.

Part II: A Proven, Groundbreaking Alternative

Jack's philosophy creates a new attitude for you

The Business of Living

When I hit the stage at one of the more than twenty seminars I do every year, this is how I introduce myself: "Hi! My name is Jack. My last name—it might as well be Inc—as in Incorporated!" And to my way of thinking, we all have that same last name—*because each one of us is a business.* One employee. Owner operated. That's because everything in life is a transaction. A deal. An act of commerce. We're just millions of little two-legged businesses buying, selling, and merging with other little two-legged businesses. I don't care who you are or what you do, you're selling something to someone.

There are two things at the top of most people's wants: Love and Money, and most of life's transactions involve one or the other. Every day of your life you are selling some aspect of yourself—it may be your ability as an employee, your sexuality to a prospective mate, indeed, your very attributes as a human being. It's reflected in our common phrases: "I'm sold on it," or, "I don't buy it." Even our popular television game shows are about transactions—"Deal or no deal?" "Let's make a deal!"

Once you are clear about this fact, life becomes very simple. Society often teaches us that success is a place where you arrive and that then your surroundings are all success-y. You even hear phrases like, "I've arrived!" or, "I've reached the pinnacle of success!" But I've never heard of a zip code for success, have you?

That's because success is not a final destination. *Success is episodic.* It's better described as you would an illness. People have *bouts* of success, a *rash* of successes, or *episodes* of success. Then success might go into remission and we flounder around again.

And if success is an episode, then the transaction is the basic measurable unit of success, and a number of successful transactions make up an episode. What I am teaching you is, *harnessing the power of immediate gratification.*

Immediate gratification gets a bad rap in psychology and sociological circles as a behavior that people need to overcome. We're taught that *deferred gratification* is far preferable as a model of human potential. But that goes against our basic instincts, as you will discover.

From Weakness Comes
Wealth

Sometimes our biggest strengths come from our weaknesses. Society teaches us to develop and emphasize our strengths and to overcome any weaknesses. But that's throwing away a huge *source of energy* within us.

Do you have any idea how many people in the world have achieved great things because their low self-esteem made them over compensate? How many people have gotten rich because they were bullied or had something to prove? People who are over-controlling have gone on to become well-known cult leaders and one could argue that Robinhood took his moral weakness as a compulsive thief to become a beloved figure in folklore. I personally know a woman who was afflicted with crippling shyness and an inability to assert herself, and she used those flaws to become the best-known submissive, or "sub" in the BDSM scene in Indianapolis, Indiana.

One night, a couple of years ago I ran into a former employee of mine in a nightclub. His name is Stevie and we spent a few minutes catching up. Then things took a turn for the serious when he told me he'd been depressed, almost suicidal. Stevie confided in me that he had a drug problem that had gone from being recreational to out-of-control.

He told me that he had a $300 dollar a day drug habit and that he spent most of his day hustling up money for his drugs.

I was quiet for a moment, then looked him straight in the eye and said, "Stevie, if you have $300 a day to spend on drugs, you're a *winner*. A winner with a slight drug problem. Think about the skill it takes for you to scrounge up all that money every day—thinking outside of the box, having to be quick on your feet. It's obvious you're a self-starter, so how can you now take all of this and get to the next level by doing something legit? I want you to think about that."

As I walked away, I thought, "Does he really know how much potential he has? I wonder how many people have a $30 a day drug habit and wish they could be in Stevie's shoes?"

If my observation seems over the top or insensitive, it's only to make a very real point. A drug addict has that singularity of purpose and laser-light focus to get more money for drugs, spending their days running around, accomplishing, achieving. Using their weaknesses to do things they never imagined they could.

The trick in life is to harness that drive but put it towards something of more lasting value.

Image

"To be a success one must first look a success."

There is a well-known "Success" speaker that loves to tell how he spent ten years hanging out with and studying the world's most successful people. He talks about how it was hard to get into their circle. He studied the habits of the Rich & Beautiful and what made them tick as though he were a scientist studying Success in its natural habitat.

Well, Jack Freeman did the opposite—I spent a decade associating with some of the biggest losers around. Believe me, it wasn't that hard to get in with those people and it was arguably a lot more fun. But more importantly, I learned a valuable lesson—one that would become an integral part of *The Business of Living*: *Hang out with losers and you'll always look like a winner.* That might sound like a no brainer, but believe me, not everyone gets it.

Image has two components: the first is how others see us, and the second is how we *want* others to see us. More often than not we want people to see us in a way that is a better version of our real self—smarter, wealthier, or sexier. Often, people don't realize that they are conveying an image in ways they never thought about.

For example, look at something as simple as your mail. You can tell a lot about someone by the *kind* of mail they get—it reflects a socioeconomic status. Take a good look at the mail that you pull from your mailbox every day. Whatever image it's conveying is due to your buying habits. Is your mail peppered with words like "cashmere", "Heirloom quality", and "investment grade", or is it riddled with terms like "polyknit", "3 EZ payments", and "street legal"? Make it a point to cultivate quality mail by sending off for expensive catalogs and subscribing to upscale magazines, (then cancelling after the first issue) and leave them out on your coffee table for visitors to see. Remember, *your mail is a demographic paper trail*—and it leads right back to you.

Let's now look at two pictures that convey iconic images and how people respond to them.

First, look at this picture of Jesus.

He has long, unkempt hair, he's wearing a houserobe, and the look on his face is one of concern or sadness. His most important message was, "I'm coming back." But we're often skeptical. Does his image convey confidence?

Now look at this picture of Arnold Schwarzenegger.

He's buff, confident—he's got guns. When he says, "I'll be back", we believe him, don't we? He *looks* like he's coming back—whether we want him to or not.

That's the power of image!

Recently, as an experiment, I stopped ten strangers on the street and asked them one question: "How much money would you estimate that I make a year?" I heard a lot of responses and the numbers ranged from $65,000 to $300,000. Actually, I made just over $54,000 last year—but I *look* like I make much more. The power of Image!

The Theory of Two-Dollar Bills

Of all my theories, none has gotten more results and acclaim than this one—The *Theory of Two-Dollar Bills*. It has shaped my image in ways you cannot imagine.

I *always* carry two-dollar bills. People are inordinately impressed with them which translates to major benefits. When you give a two-dollar bill to somebody, they look at it like it's a big deal because they're rarely seen. Let's say you go into a coffee shop. You get an order of toast and coffee. The bill comes to a dollar ninety. You leave a two-dollar bill on the table. The waitress is so intrigued with the duece that she doesn't even notice you've only left a dime tip. I'm not saying you should under-tip—but you see where the opportunities are, right? It's the same with a valet. I pull my car up to an upscale hotel, the valet opens my car door and I push a two-dollar bill into his hand. He glances at it and almost always exclaims, "Oh, nice!"

as he runs off to show his co-workers. I guarantee you that your car will be parked close by and you won't have to wait for it.

The bill holds a lot of mystique. You give one to the average Joe, he thinks you're some kind of insider—*he perceives you as having clout.* The first question I invariably get is, "Wow, where'd you get *this*?" Like I must know someone with connections. It never occurs to people that they can just go to the bank and ask a teller for some. And if the bank has none you can get them to order twos from the Federal Reserve—takes three days and costs you nothing. Then you usually get *consecutive serial numbers*, which is a whole different story.

Strip clubs. I *always* use twos in strip clubs. You see, when you're tossing money up on the stage in the dark, they tend to look like a twenty. So what happens? Now the stripper is paying more attention to *you.* Even when she finally notices it's only a two, she's still thinking, "Hmm, this guys *different*, he's not like the others—*I like him.*" Big plus.

But the bottom line here is simply that people *remember* you. The next time the person you gave one to sees you, though they may not recall what it is about you, they invariably think to themselves, "I remember that guy is somehow different. He made an impression on me—I like him!"

You see that face on there? It might as well be *yours.*

Leave your mark on this world any and every way you can!

The Fear of Loss Theory

I'm sure you've heard the phrase, "fear of success" or "fear of failure", but for the first time ever, I am going to let you in on a powerful concept that no one until me, has let you in on—known as The Fear of Loss Theory.

The Fear of Loss Theory states that *the fear of loss is stronger than the desire to gain.*

Think about that for a moment. Can you think of times in your life when you were afraid to reach for something better, electing to hold on to something undesirable because you feared the possibility of being left with nothing? Maybe you've stayed in a bad relationship, not daring to seek a better partner because your mind kept telling you, "I don't want to chance losing him even though he's abusive—I may not find anyone better!"

The fear of loss is stronger than the desire to gain.

Do you know why I'm always able to drive a new car? Because I understand—and have overcome—the Fear of Loss and use it in unique ways. Let me explain.

I know that I could never put aside my quarters and dollars until I've eventually saved up for a new car. You could say I'm impatient or that I don't understand deferred gratification. Whatever the reason, *my desire to gain is not that strong*.

So instead I just go out and get the new car I want even if it's not a good financial decision. The car dealer lets me (or anyone for that matter) give them a small down payment, I lie about my income, sign the papers for something that I can't afford, and drive my new car off the lot. Immediately, the dynamics of my theory start kicking in.

I've elevated my lifestyle, I suddenly appear more success-ful. People's heads turn in wondrous envy as I zoom by. I'm more desirable to women because I look like a winner. And all of that dynamic comes together to create in me the fear of loss. *I don't want to lose this newfound status!* The fear of losing that car now motivates me to keep up the payments no matter what. Maybe I have to cut back on child support, maybe I'm forced to switch to generic cigarettes. But I've raised my stan-dard of living and accomplished to what most people can only dream about.

How can you use the Fear of Loss in *your* life?

Optimism

Optimism is standing in a field of shit and being confident that there's a pony nearby. —Jack Freeman

Here's a favorite joke of mine:

"Knock knock."

"Who's there?"

"Opportunity"

"Opportunity who?"

"Why do you question opportunity when it's right in front of you?"

I'm always shocked that people don't see opportunity, but then most people aren't very optimistic. Below, is an actual conversation between myself and a former girlfriend.

> Dorinda: *Jack, you have no healthcare insurance! What if you fall and break your leg??*
>
> Me: *I worry more about getting impaled on a white picket fence.*

>Dorinda: *And you have no pension! Where's your pension? My dad had a nice pension—worked hard, retired, got a pension!*
>
>Me: *But he died two months after he retired.*
>
>Dorinda: *Yeah, but at least he had a pension! Look at you—you're alive but have no pension—you might as well be dead!*

She was always the voice of doom and gloom. For Dorinda, "Happy Hour" lasted about ten minutes. She had no optimism.

The French philosopher Voltaire defined optimism as: "The mania of maintaining that everything is well when we are wretched." Well, if optimism is a mania, then I must be a maniac. And I hope to make one out of you too!

When I go out onstage to do one of my seminars I usually haven't seen the audience yet. If I walk out there and a third of the seats are empty, my first words to the audience are, "How many people here see 300 empty seats? Because I don't. I see 300 people that aren't ready for success and 65 that are!"

Part III: Building Your Business From the Ground Up

Concrete ideas for getting ahead

The Yard Sale

"Caveat emptor."

I love yard sales. There is nothing more American than the classic yard sale. The yard sale represents the purest form of entrepreneurial business. It's the petri dish of capitalism.

Nothing will better train you for the Business of Living than a yard sale and it's simple to have one—you don't even need a yard. You just need to know someone with one, ideally that someone is wealthy with a circular driveway. A*nyone* can make money with a yard sale and that's what this chapter is going to show you how to do.

Rule Number One about yard sales: *You can sell whatever you want, for whatever price you can get.* And most importantly, the Consumer Protection laws don't cover yard sales! There is no three-day cooling off period in Jack Freeman's world.

This is also the perfect time to teach your children the only latin phrase they ever need to know: *"Caveat Emptor"*, which means, *let the buyer beware.*

First off, there's a whole method to a yard sale. You don't even want think of it as your yard—it's a showroom! It's your sales floor! So you don't just strew your belongings out on the lawn. How many times have you seen a yard sale, the stuff is strewn all over—it looks like you've come upon the result of a domestic dispute. You want make aisles, you want to break it up into departments, or else people will root through your stuff like Calcuttans scavenging through a landfill.

Second, success at your yard sale doesn't just happen. There has to be *action* behind it.

You've probably held a yard sale before. What did you do? You got your items out of the house and then you put price tags on the stuff, poured a cup of coffee, and sat down on a chair waiting for people to come by.

No No No!

You see, most people having a yard sale make that mistake. They just sit there like a spectator. *Impotent to the success of their own event.* They're simply *hoping* someone will come along and maybe buy something.

Friend, *make the deal happen!* That stuff doesn't just sell itself—do whatever you've gotta do to move the stuff! Remember, the consumer protection laws do not apply to yard sales. And if everything in your life is a transaction—a deal—then that makes you a salesman, and what does a salesman do? He sells. He takes the initiative!

One of the tricks to a yard sale is to have *loss leaders*. Take something valuable out of your house, like expensive binoculars. (Don't worry, you aren't actually going to sell them.) Put a big price sticker on it for $8. Then, right next to it put a big "SOLD" sticker on it. When people see a couple of items that are obviously undervalued, they unconsciously assume *everything's* under priced.

Next, always have a non-existent partner. It let's you create a "good cop/bad cop" situation that puts you on the side of the buyer. Here's an example of *You* in action:

You: (to buyer) "How much do I want for the espresso machine? Oh, that's not mine—It's my buddy's. He wants $80 for it."

Buyer: "Oh never mind—it's way overpriced."

You: "I agree. I told him that but, he's in a hospice, he's not always thinking clearly nowadays. ...If only he'd had insurance..."

(At this point, read the buyers face. If that exchange didn't make him buy it, go to this next step.)

You: "Tell you what, let me call him and see if he'll come down some."

(Step away, but stay close enough for buyer to hear you and make fake phone call to partner.)

You: "Tim? Hey it's me. Listen I have someone here who—what? I'm sorry, I know the transfusions must be really painful. Listen, someone wants to buy your espresso machine but they think it's—yeah, I understand ... they give you a little bucket to keep next to the bed?

Buyer, interrupting: "That's Okay, I'll give you $80 for it. Don't ask him to come down on it."

You: "You will? Aww, thanks, you made his day—and God knows he doesn't have many of them."

If someone doesn't buy the item after an exchange like that, *it's not your fault*. Occasionally you'll run into people that are so heartless that there's just no getting through to them.

There are a million tips I can pass on but here are some of the more useful ones:

Don't provide access to electricity! Anything electronic like dvr's, flatscreens, vacuum cleaners, will subject to nitpicking by buyers If they want to know if it works, just say, "As far as I know..."

Sometimes I hear people say to themselves, "I don't have enough stuff to justify a yard sale." You should not define your yard sale by "stuff that I owned and no longer have use for." That's not thinking outside of the box. Your yard sale is a place for *resale,* meaning you should always be on the lookout for sources of product such as other people's yard sales, Goodwill donation boxes and warehouses that receive recalled products from manufacturers are especially good places to look.

You've heard the business saying, "Buy low, sell high." That to me, is a little simplistic. You will be more focused towards success if instead you remember, "You make your money when you buy, not when you sell."

Pricing. There are two lines of thought here. The first is to always have price tags on your goods. When someone sees a tag, they're less likely to try to negotiate—especially WASPs. The other theory is to have no price on an item, similar to how used car lots operate. By having no price, it lets you size up your prospective buyer's naivete, intelligence, or financial worth. Remember: we are all little two-legged businesses!

Don't you judge brick and mortar stores for your shopping decisions? You should look at people the same way—are they a strip mall type or an anchor store?

Did you know that it's legal to sell guns at yard sales? You should strongly consider having an inventory of high margin firearms. Most people have no real idea of a gun's worth so it's best to have cheaper, low-quality guns for sale. Try to have guns that are nickel plated or stainless steel since they glint in the sunlight and catch people's eye.

Remember the saying, "One man's trash is another man's treasure"? Your goal is to make sure someone is treasuring the trash that you just sold them.

And finally, do you know what the most common items for sale at yard sales are? Exercise equipment—treadmills, lifecycles, weights, and other fitness items like yoga mats, smoking cessation programs, and Success-Inspirational-Motivation books. What do all these have in common? *They are all items geared towards achievement.*

Do you think that people are selling these things because they achieved their goals and no longer have any need for them? Or, have they realized that they can't "achieve the impossible" and have instead opted for the *attainable*?

12

Carpe Opportunum!

"I don't care if you're broke. Being in the red is just a pigment of your imagination."
—Jack Freeman

How many times have you found yourself standing over your child's piggy bank, hammer raised above your head, tears streaming down your face, and thought, "There's got to be a better way."

Well, this next chapter is going to show you a better way. The chapter title describes our new mindset—*Carpe Opportunum*, a Peruvian phrase meaning, "Seize the Opportunity". The Business of Living emphasizes spotting opportunities and turning them into successful exchanges.

Let's talk for a moment about location. I want you to think about the times you've gone to a mall. When you walk through a mall, you're essentially on a street, and you turn off of the "street" to go left or right into a store. But what I want you to notice are the kiosks that run down the center of mall. The kiosks typically sell smaller, affordable items, often impulse buys and the salespeople usually call out to you as you pass. The kiosks are simply a modern version of the street bazaars and marketplaces that began in the Middle East and are still successful. I have long admired the mall kiosks as the perfect example of The Business of Living's philosophy. A one person, two-legged business that's right in the mix of things! Who has a better chance of selling something to you—the bored salesgirl standing way in the back of a jewelry store or the guy who's in the middle of hundreds of people walking by and treating his kiosk like a yard sale? Always put yourself in the middle of crowds—*you're that much closer to their wallet.*

*

To get you started, I'm providing you with some of my moneymaking ideas that are tried and true. I have personally used these to make thousands, if not hundreds of dollars—and now you can too. Remember, The Business of Living is always about success and success is all about transactions, and the following, is one of my favorites.

This transaction is also one of the easiest. I call it, "Kittens to a good home." If you go to a laundromat, library, or coffeehouse, they will usually have bulletin boards and you'll see tons of notices that say, *"Kittens—free to a good home."* I gather all these notices and then collect up all the kittens that I can—and I sell them for $10 a piece.

But the key here is to *get the whole litter.* It's not worth your time and gas money to schlep around getting one kitten here and another one halfway across town. So I have a little phone presentation that I use when I call the number. Something along the lines of, "I'm with a volunteer organization that provides pets for veterans and the elderly in retirement homes..."

Add a line in there like, "If you could see how their faces light up when they first hold their kitten..."

Once, you've collected up at least fifteen to twenty kittens, you're ready to go to work. Now, who is typically your target market for kittens? It's women and kids. So you want to set up in front of a mall or maybe near a McDonald's entrance. I put them in a large box. You want them to able to move around because the more they can frolic, the cuter they look, the faster they sell. And I mix them up. I'll put in a Siamese, a calico, a grey. *But no more than four in the box or people can't make up their minds.* Remember—you can always go back to the car for more. I price them at $10, and tell people, "I have to sell them today or they go to the animal research lab." On a good day I can move thirty-five or forty kittens. And I'm betting you can do even better!

So, let's analyze the above. The Kitten Scheme works so well because it's structured around one of the strongest motivators in Man: *emotion.* We use emotion to sell at every turn in the above scenario, beginning with targeting women and children who are particularly susceptible. Then, the use of emotion-packed words like "veteran," "elderly," and "volunteer." Even the use of an oversized, large box to hold the kittens is deliberate. A large box makes the kittens appear smaller—almost as if they're in a hole or a well. Additionally, their meowing echos more in a big box. And of course, the term, "animal research" is a highly emotional one. The Kittens Scheme is not genius, it's simply a case of thinking outside of the box and creating wealth through simple transactions.

*

Bitcoin. This is a new currency that I had to get my head around because the average person knows little about it and doesn't really understand how it works. Which makes it perfect for us! Remember, *In confusion, there's profit*. Bitcoin is bought and sold over the internet. Below is an official picture of Bitcoin.

Many people think that this is what a bitcoin looks like. But get this—*It is entirely a digital currency and doesn't exist in the physical world.* Yes, that's confusing, but here's how you profit from that confusion. If you go on Ebay, you can buy one of these "coins" for about $6. They are heavy and surprisingly well made. Bitcoin trades online and currently the price is $10,250. For one bitcoin. You see where we're going with this?!

As an experiment, I went to downtown Cincinnati and stopped a few pedestrians and said, "Listen, I've got a bitcoin on me and I am really in need of money." (At this point, I pull it out to show them.) "Look, I'm desperate—the going price right now for bitcoin is $10,000—you can look it up on your phone right now." (Let them look it up on their phone so they trust the number.) Then tell them, "I'd take $3000 for this right now. Here, hold it, it's real."

Out of eight people I stopped, only one told me to get screwed. Three others were interested but had no funds. *But four of the eight were willing to go to their ATM or bank to take advantage of this once-in-a-lifetime deal!* People have never "seen" a bitcoin and are convinced that currency must have a physical structure. I won't tell you how many bitcoins I sold, but trust me, I made money. Let me know how you fare at this rare opportunity!

*

I often tell the next anecdote at my seminars. It's about the power of perception as it pertains to marketing.

A while back, I was at a party where most of the guests were a really straight-laced bunch. I was in a bathroom and had just pulled a vial of cocaine out of my pocket when a guy burst in, thinking it was unoccupied. "Geez, sorry!" he said. He turned to leave but stopped and asked, "What's that?" pointing to the vial of coke in my hand.

Thinking quickly, I said, "Oh, it an energy powder that I sometimes take when I'm losing steam."

He introduced himself as Glenn, then asked, "Mind if I try a little? I just put in a fifteen-hour day at the office."

"Uh, sure, I guess so," I said, a little taken aback. I showed Glenn how to pour a little on the back of his hand and sniff it.

Glenn stood up after a moment and exclaimed, "Wow, this stuff really perks you up! What's in it?"

I handed him the vial saying, "It's all natural. It comes from a plant in South America."

Glenn examined the vial, then asked, "Are you a distributor for this energy powder? Can I buy some?"

I laughed, and told him to give me his phone number and a sales rep would be in touch.

Glenn asked to have one last "sniff" and as he walked away he said, "I know a ton of people that would like this new energy powder!"

I have a knack for seeing opportunities in everyday situations but you can develop this skill too just by adhering to my philosophy and finding ways to "pick the lock."

*

Okay, so let's say you've done a lot of quick, "in-and-out" transactions, have made some money and now want to start a small business. One of your biggest expenses will be employees. But what if I told you you could have five or even ten employees *for free*—that's right, a workforce of your own that costs you nothing! Listen up!

There's a little known sexual subculture called "submissives". These "subs," as we call them in the business, are part of a whole scene. You can find these people at underground clubs, in chat rooms, or on specialized dating sites.

These are people that for whatever reason, like to be dominated and ordered around. *They get sexual gratification from this.* You'll find these people that actually *like* to be ordered around, demeaned, and made to do unsavory things. This is where it gets interesting and profitable because it's an easy leap to get them to do the work that your business is engaged in, whether it's assembling product in your manufacturing operation or cleaning toilets for your janitorial company. Remember, they like to get down and dirty and many subs like being forced to wear confining masks—so if you need welding done, they're perfect. And remember, the harder you work them the happier they are! Their pain is your gain. Some people would call that slavery—I call it an *alternative energy source*.

Let me take a moment to say that I'm aware that a minority of readers might think that some of my ideas are a little "out there". That's understandable—people tend to be resistant to new ways of thinking until they see a logic in it. Let me close this chapter with something for you to think about.

Recently, I watched an older movie titled *Indecent Proposal*. It starred Woody Harrelson and Demi Moore as a married couple down on their luck. A wealthy businessman comes along and offers a million dollars if he can sleep with the man's wife. Well, at this point in the film I had to roll my eyes. I'm sure none of us could get a million dollars for someone to sleep with our wife—*but we could get twenty dollars, fifty thousand times*.

How often we overlook the obvious, but this should spur you into finding new ways to look at situations in order to find the opportunities within. Remember, *you don't need the key to success if you know how to pick the lock.*

13

Bonus Section! - The Business of Loving

Last year, I was having a drink in the lounge at The Hampton Inn of Dubuque (maybe you've seen pictures of it—it was recently written up in *Trailways* magazine). I had finished giving a seminar a few hours earlier and now sat sipping a cordial, looking out over the city. I lived in a nine-hundred-dollar-a-month penthouse, I owned two cars both under three-years-old, and would likely make over $80k by year's end. *I had it made.*

But I felt empty somehow. There had to be more to life than this. As I sat listening to the pop music coming over the lounge's sound system, I had a revelation: Almost all of the songs on the radio are about Love. People do crazy things in the name of love—people even commit suicide over it! The Beatles went so far to say all you need is love. The answer was right in front of me! Why couldn't I apply the Business of Living philosophy to personal relationships? *What if it could put your love life in the black?*

Introducing: The Business of Loving, which teaches that, *all personal relationships are simply transactions*—and the currency of these transactions is *expectation*.

Take a second and look at the person you're in a relationship with. In that exchange, who got the best end of the deal? Do you ever say to yourself, "He was no bargain", or "She sold me a bill of goods." Are you experiencing buyer's remorse?

Maybe you're married—a merger. How's that venture going? Have there been "violations of the terms of the contract?"

What is a one night stand but an "impulse buy." And the next morning, when you say to yourself, "He just used me and threw me away," didn't you sell yourself as disposable?

You see, it's no wonder that relationships can't and don't work! Because they're *ongoing*. You have to sell yourself to that person everyday. And who can live up to their own warranty?

I wrote earlier about yard sales. In the context of personal relationships, that's really what you are—a walking, talking yard sale, an assortment of everything you've amassed over the years, your entire collection of memories and experiences. If you want to know who you truly are, look at what's spread out on the Lawn of your Life. And it's all for sale isn't it? Because everyone's looking for Love.

And Love is just getting someone to buy your stuff. Your personal inventory. Your emotional bric-a-brac. I'll bet that under your bed you have a shoe box full of old Hallmark cards and dried bunches of roses—aren't those just Love's receipts? Do you keep them as Proof of Purchase?

Let's look at some specifics. When you're selling something to someone there are only three approaches. You appeal to either their *fear,* their *greed,* or their *desire for exclusivity.* Everything from perfume to Ponzi schemes is based on this, and it's the same with love.

In our youth, we sell ourselves to the opposite sex based on their Desire for Exclusivity by intimating that, *I'm unique. I'm one-of-a-kind. I'm special.*

But then time passes. Maybe you don't find a suitable buyer. Maybe you're lonely. So you start selling yourself a little cheaper. What signs are in your window now?

Marked down for quick sale.

Big Savings on last year's model!

I will not be undersold!

You're selling them with your fear.

Or maybe you spot a bargain. Someone who looks like a good turnaround opportunity. "With a little time and effort, I can create value here. So what he has a drug problem, so what he has no ambition, no self-esteem? I can turn this deal around! Get a good return on my emotional investment." But your currency was expectation and you find he's always operating in the red, the balance sheet's unbalanced.

Then you start to think maybe you're the faulty product. "Maybe I put too much value on myself." You come to realize that selling kittens or guns is easy compared to selling yourself. So it's easier to take yourself off the market, thus avoiding the scrutiny of a potential buyer.

If my treatment of the Business of Loving seems negative or cynical, it's only to prove my point. The marketplace of Love was not designed for brick and mortar operations with it's time cards and costly overhead. Instead, it operates best as a temporary kiosk, or yes, a yard sale. Since this is a new application of my existing philosophy, I cannot yet vouch to its effectiveness, though I can say that I've been in nine relationships in just the last two years and I'm confident that you can achieve those kinds of numbers in your life!

About the Author

Jack Freeman has given motivational seminars since 1997. He's headlined the renowned *Successapalooza* Tour for six years and though forced to take time off for three years, he is now back on the road helping everyday people get ahead in life. A member of numerous professional organizations, Jack regularly speaks at both AA and Gamblers Anonymous meetings. He recently founded a success program, *Little Winners* to help children get a jump start on life. *The Business of Living* is his first book.